Centre for Public Health Research

D1745532

Sure Start Blacc

Engaging with fam

'hard to

Fiona Ward

Miranda Thurston

August 2006

Acknowledgements

There are a number of people who we would like to thank for their involvement in this piece of research:

- the parents who shared their views and experiences with us;

- Frances Mann at the Centre for Public Health Research for conducting some of the interviews and contributing to the report;

- the administration staff at Sure Start Blacon;

- John Zlosnik, Senior Lecturer in Computer Science and Information Systems at the University of Chester for his assistance in extracting the information from the database.

This research was commissioned and funded by Sure Start Blacon.

Contents

Page

Acknowledgements   i

Contents   ii

Tables   v

Figures   vi

Summary   vii

Chapter 1   **Introduction**   1

1.1   Sure Start local programmes   1

1.2   Sure Start Blacon   1

1.3   The aim of the study   1

1.4   Ethics   2

1.5   The structure of the report   2

Chapter 2   **Programme Reach**   3

2.1   Introduction   3

2.2   Programme reach   3

2.3   'Hard to reach' families   8

2.4   'Hard to reach' services   9

Chapter 3   **Study design and methods**   11

3.1   Introduction   11

3.2   The sample   11

3.3   The interviews   13

3.4   Interview analysis   13

Chapter 4   **Findings**   14

4.1   Introduction   14

4.2   Family information   14

4.3   Current routines   16

4.3.1   Work and childcare   16

4.3.2   School nursery and pre-school   17

4.3.3   Activities and groups   18

4.3.4   Meeting with family and friends   18

4.3.5	Time at home and household tasks	18
4.4	Knowledge about and use of Sure Start Blacon	19
4.4.1	Getting to know about Sure Start	19
4.4.2	Publicity and information	19
4.4.3	Using activities and services	20
4.4.3.1	Mother and child experiences	22
4.4.3.2	Group dynamics	23
4.4.3.3	Sure Start workers	23
4.4.3.4	The venues	24
4.5	Barriers to service use	24
4.6	Possible solutions	28
4.7	Blacon Hall Children's Centre	30
4.8	Interest in existing activities	30
4.8.1	Adult education	31
4.8.2	Pop In	32
4.8.3	Song, Story and Rhymetime	32
4.9	Further contact and overall interest in Sure Start Blacon	33
Chapter 5	**Discussion**	**36**
5.1	Introduction	36
5.2	Knowing the local population	36
5.3	Understanding parents' priorities and changing behaviour	37
5.4	Responding to working parents	38
5.5	Programme priorities	39
5.5.1	Targeting	39
5.5.2	Information	40
5.5.3	Working with mainstream services	40
5.5.4	Outreach and welcoming services	41
Chapter 6	**Conclusions**	**43**
6.1	Introduction	43
6.2	The methodology and sample	43
6.3	Diversity of families who are hard to reach	44
6.4	An acceptable level of non-involvement	45
6.5	The implications for Sure Start and children's centres	46
References		**48**

Appendices

Appendix 1   Ranking of deprivation   47

Appendix 2   Letter for respondents   51

Appendix 3   Information sheet   53

Appendix 4   Interview schedule   56

Appendix 5   Consent form   65

Tables

		Page
Table 3.2.1	Reason for non-response	12
Table 4.2.1	Age of mother	14
Table 4.2.2	Age of children	15
Table 4.2.3	Time resident in the Blacon area	16
Table 4.3.1.1	Childcare used by working mothers	17
Table 4.4.3.1	Sure Start services accessed by parents	22
Table 4.5.1	Barriers reported by respondents	25
Table 4.6.1	Solutions to identified barriers	29
Table 4.9.1	Further information or contact with Sure Start	33

Figures

Page

Figure 2.2.1   Sure Start Blacon service users (Oct. 05 – Mar. 06)   5

Figure 2.2.2   Sure Start Blacon lead carers not using services (Oct. 05 – Mar. 06)   6

Figure 2.2.3   Families interviewed as part of the research   7

Figure 4.5.1   Extent to which barriers applied to respondents   27

Figure 4.8.1   Interest expressed in specific Sure Start Blacon activities   31

Summary

Why we did the research

Although Sure Start Blacon has tried to make sure that all parents and carers know about the activities offered by the programme, some families do not use their services. Sure Start Blacon wanted to find out more about the things that prevented families from coming to their activities and to see if there were things they could do to encourage them to attend.

What did we do?

The names of 137 families who had not attended any Sure Start Blacon activities for six months were taken from the database. Each family was sent a letter to explain about the research and to ask them to take part. During April and May 2006, 31 interviews were completed (a response rate of 23%). The interviews were conducted by researchers from the University of Chester and took place in the families' homes: all of the interviews were with mothers, although dads/partners were present on three occasions.

What did we find?

Family information
Mums aged in their thirties and forties accounted for 77% (24) of the people interviewed – only seven mums were aged 29 years or younger. The majority of the parents interviewed had lived in Blacon for more than 20 years - only one mum had lived there for less than two years and all of the parents had been living in the Sure Start Blacon area when their youngest child was born. The 31 families contained 67 children, 33 of whom were aged under four: two mums were also expecting a baby. Although most families had only one young child, four families had two children of Sure Start age.

Current routines
Almost three quarters (22) of the mums were employed or at college. Four mums worked or studied full-time whilst 18 worked on a part-time basis. Seven of the mothers who worked part-time did so in the evening, at night or at weekends. Only four

mums who worked did not rely on dads/partners or other family members for their childcare.

The research found that 19 of the 27 children who were two or three years old went to a school nursery or pre-school. Eight children attended a group activity during the week that was not organised by Sure Start. Some mums said that they had never looked for groups that they could go to with their children whilst others had tried them but their child was unhappy in the activity. Four parents said they were just starting to think about looking for an activity that their child could go to or they could attend with them.

When families were asked about the other things they did during the week, seven mums talked about time spent with family and friends, especially those who also had younger children. Six people mentioned time at home doing household jobs and 10 talked about activities they did in or around the home such as crafts, playing, cycling, walks and play-centre or library visits. Some parents also said that they spent time at home because their children were tired after nursery or pre-school or that they did not feel that their child needed to be at groups and activities everyday. Some parents who worked said that they just wanted to spend time alone with their children or just needed to catch up with things. There were, however, three mums who were with their young children all day who did not go to any groups and did not describe any activities that they did with their children at home.

Knowledge about and use of Sure Start Blacon

Most of the mums first heard about Sure Start Blacon when they were pregnant or soon after their children were born, usually from a midwife or health visitor. All of the families had received information about Sure Start activities through the post. They were generally positive about the style and content of the information but a third of the families said they now received less information than they had done in the past.

All of the parents described at least one contact they had had with Sure Start Blacon, either a home visit or at an activity. Twenty-five people said that they had had a home visit from a Sure Start worker. They were generally positive about the home visits and some comments were made about how friendly the staff were and how much information they had been given.

Seven parents said that they had not used any Sure Start activities and three had been to local activities with their children but they were not sure if they were organised by

Sure Start or someone else. The Sure Start activities that had been attended most in the past were baby massage, Song, Story and Rhymetime and the Pop In. Some parents had positive experiences of the activities whilst others said that their children had not enjoyed them, that they found the groups cliquey or the venues uncomfortable.

Barriers to service use

During the interview, families were asked about the things that had stopped them from attending Sure Start Blacon activities. The most frequently mentioned reason was a lack of time, usually because of work. Also important was having someone to go with or knowing other parents who attend and, often linked to that, were mums who did not feel comfortable in the groups or felt that activities were cliquey and it was difficult to join in. The timing of activities and picking up and dropping off children at school, nursery or pre-school was a problem for some parents and some said that their children were too tired to go to another group once they had spent half of the day at pre-school or nursery. One mum said that they did not attend Sure Start activities because it was not relevant to her and another had been put off by a bad experience at a group. Seven parents, however, said that they preferred their own routine or wanted to spend time alone with their children whilst others felt that once their child started attending pre-school or school nursery they did not need Sure Start activities.

When mums were given a list of things that other people had said might stop them from using Sure Start, 68% (21) agreed that time was a problem, 48% (15) said not knowing anyone who goes stopped them and 39% (12) said not knowing about the activities was a barrier. Also important, but affecting a smaller number of mums, was not knowing where the places were, not being bothered, activities seen as being irrelevant and a lack of confidence.

Possible solutions

When asked if Sure Start could do anything to make it easier for them to get involved, 13 mums said that there was nothing that Sure Start Blacon could do. Suggestions made by other parents included changes to the timing of activities, more information, different venues and having ways of introducing new people to the group.

Interest in existing activities

Three existing Sure Start Blacon activities (adult education, the Pop In and Song, Story and Rhymetime) were described to the parents to show the range of Sure Start Blacon's services and to find out if they might be interested in attending in the future.

Of the 31 parents who were interviewed, five were certain that they would not be going to any of these activities. Where mums were interested, Song, Story and Rhymetime was the most popular, followed by adult education courses. Fewest parents were interested in attending the Pop In.

Future contact with Sure Start Blacon

At the end of the interview, parents were asked if they would like someone from Sure Start Blacon to contact them to tell them more about any activities. Twenty-two mums said they would like some contact or more information and these requests were passed on the Sure Start Blacon soon after the interviews were completed.

What does this mean for Sure Start Blacon?

The Sure Start local programme in Blacon has now become a Children's Centre. The findings from this research present a range of issues that Sure Start Blacon can consider as they put together their local Children's Centre delivery plan.

- The Children's Centre needs to have an accurate database of children and families and simple systems so that they can record who is and who is not using services.

- It is also necessary to keep some additional information so that families who have said that want to use Sure Start or who have particular needs that Sure Start can meet can be identified and the right kind of service can be offered to them.

- The circumstances and situation of each family will change over time and Sure Start needs to work in partnership with other agencies so that families can get in touch with services when they want or need them.

- Sure Start needs to imagine how each of their activities looks from the viewpoint of local families and to consider how families will hear about services, what information they need before they decide to attend and what it might feel like to a parent who is going for the first time.

- Some services may need to be designed specifically for families who find it hard to get involved at the moment and different ways should be tried to encourage them.

- Services must be presented and advertised so that all local families with young children understand that activities are provided for people like them.

- Sure Start needs to be there in the background even when families do not seem to want to be involved so that parents know how to contact them if they choose to.

- When families who have not used services at all or who have not used them for a long time show an interest in an activity, Sure Start needs to be able to respond and help the family get involved straight away.

- Many parents work and Sure Start must consider what they provide for fathers, grandparents and other people who care for young children during the day and whether or not there is a demand from working parents for certain types of services in the evenings or at weekends.

- All services should to be welcoming and Sure Start workers need to make sure that new families feel comfortable when they go to an activity for the first time.

Chapter 1

Introduction

1.1 Sure Start local programmes

Sure Start was established in 1998 by the Labour Government following a Comprehensive Spending Review. The aim of the initiative was to improve the health and wellbeing of children and families who lived in the most disadvantaged areas of the country so that children were 'ready to thrive' when they started school. By 2005, there were 524 Sure Start local programmes in operation nationally, serving approximately 400,000 children.

The four Sure Start objectives were to improve social and emotional development, to improve health, to improve children's ability to learn and to strengthen families and communities. These objectives were to be achieved by bringing together agencies working in education, health, social welfare and the voluntary sector to work in innovative ways to offer improved and needs-focused services to all children and families in their area.

1.2 Sure Start Blacon

Sure Start Blacon is a fourth round programme that was established in 2002. Blacon is located within the City of Chester and the Sure Start area includes all of the Blacon Hall and Dee Point wards and a small part of the Sealand ward.

The lead agency for the Blacon programme was the voluntary organisation, NCH. Since April 2006, however, Cheshire County Council has become the lead agency and accountable body in preparation for the move to a children's centre. Blacon Hall Children Centre is one of Cheshire's phase one centres, to be opened in September 2006. The initial reach of the Centre will be the 850 children aged nought to four years in the Sure Start catchment area but this will be extended to 1,100 children as the Centre becomes integrated into Cheshire's universal Children's Centre programme.

1.3 The aim of the study

The focus of this study is to understand the experiences of a group of families who have not accessed services provided by the Sure Start local programme in Blacon. The aim of the study is to identify and explore the factors which have affected the

willingness and ability of individuals to engage with Sure Start Blacon services. Whilst both barriers and incentives to securing participation were explored, the research also attempted to understand the complexity of the factors, both individual and contextual, which influence how families use local services and how these factors may change over time.

The objectives of the research were to find out more about what has prevented people from becoming involved in Sure Start Blacon, to understand the needs of families who do not access Sure Start services and to identify what could be put in place to enable more families to become involved.

1.4   Ethics

Ethical issues are covered under an existing ethics application to the South Cheshire Local Research Ethics Committee, which was approved in December 2003 and runs until October 2006.

1.5   The structure of the report

Chapter 2 explores the issue of programme reach and examines the definitions of 'hard to reach'. Chapter 3 describes the methodology of this piece of work and Chapter 4 presents the findings from the interviews. Chapter 5 includes a discussion of the main findings and Chapter 6 considers the implications for Sure Start Blacon and the new children's centre.

Chapter 2

Programme Reach

2.1 Introduction

Sure Start services were established to be available to all children under four years old and their families living in the catchment area. The Sure Start Unit asks local programmes for monitoring information 'to show that you are reaching your intended population, especially those groups that are potentially the hardest to reach and most in need of Sure Start services" (Sure Start Unit, 2002, para.4.16). This chapter describes the current reach of the Sure Start Blacon local programme and explores the concept of 'hard to reach'.

2.2 Programme reach

There are approximately 740 families with children under the age of four years living in the Sure Start Blacon area (Ward, Alford, Thurston, & Pearson, 2006). Parents-to-be and families with children aged nought to three years old are eligible to be registered with the programme and, if they do so, this information is put onto a computerised database. In March 2006, 375 eligible families with children under the age of four years were registered with the programme.

Also entered onto the database each month are attendance lists for all Sure Start Blacon services: in this way, the number of registered children and parents who attend activities can be monitored for the programme's own information and to send to the Sure Start Unit. Information about adults and children who live in Blacon but are not registered cannot be entered onto the database and so their attendance cannot be monitored in the same way.

An extract from the database, taken in March 2006, showed that 207 of the 375 registered families with children under the age of four years had used at least one service during the previous six months: the remaining 168 families (45%) had not attended any Sure Start Blacon service at all.

Through the use of geographical information systems (GIS) it is possible to present a spatial representation of the information from the Sure Start Blacon database. The following maps illustrate the distribution of families who are registered with Sure Start

by their postcode area. The first shows families where the lead carer had used a Sure Start Blacon service during the six months prior to the research (Figure 2.2.1) and the second map shows those who had not used a service in the previous six months and so formed the main sample for the research (Figure 2.2.2). The third map (Figure 2.2.3) shows the location of the 31 parents who were interviewed during the research.

The background on the maps shows super output areas (SOA), shaded to indicate their ranking within Cheshire on a number of indicators of deprivation. The index of deprivation includes seven criteria: these are income, employment, health deprivation and disability, education, skills and training, barriers to housing and services, crime and disorder, and the living environment (Cheshire County Council, 2006).

The key in Appendix 1 shows all of the ranking categories: the areas that make up the Blacon Sure Start area are ranked in the first seven bands (a SOA ranking 106 and below). The darker green shading, and the lower numbers on the scale, indicates the areas that are ranked higher in the index of deprivation.

The maps show that both service users and families who have not accessed Sure Start Blacon services are distributed throughout the area. This is also the case for the families who were interviewed as part of the research: whilst some lived in the areas of the ward that were ranked lower on the index of deprivation, some families also lived in the higher ranked areas. The maps also show the location of the new Sure Start Children's Centre in Blacon.

Figure 2.2.1   Sure Start Blacon service users (Oct. 05 – Mar. 06)

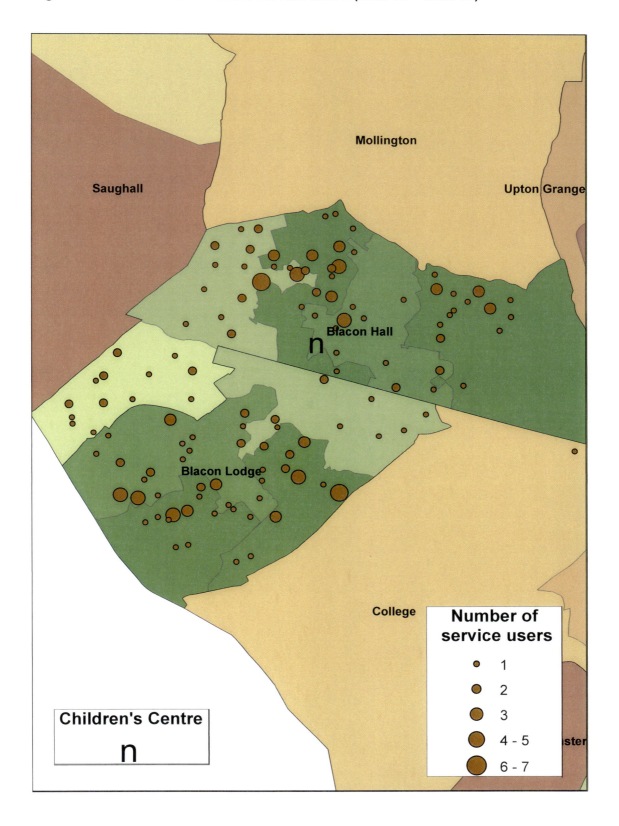

Figure 2.2.2   Sure Start Blacon lead carers not using services (Oct. 05 – Mar. 06)

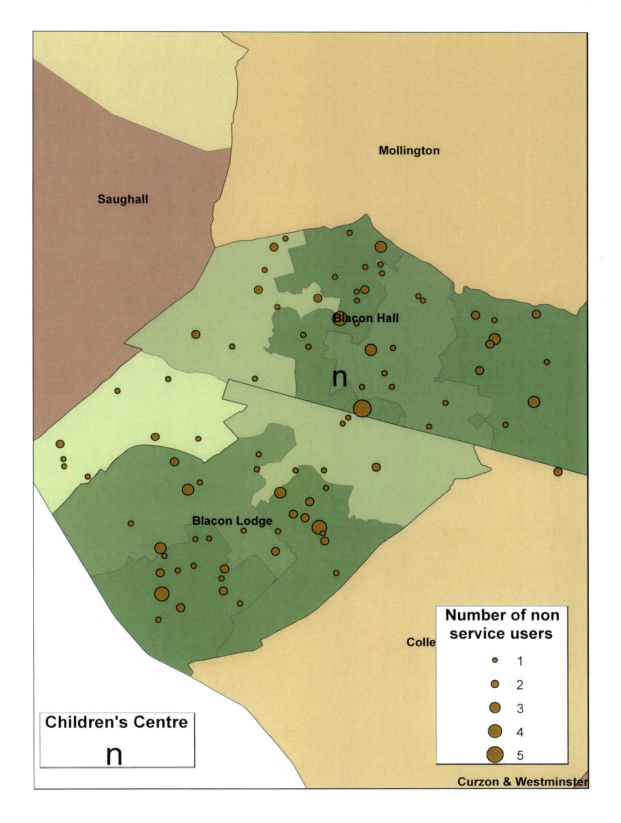

Figure 2.2.3   Families interviewed as part of the research

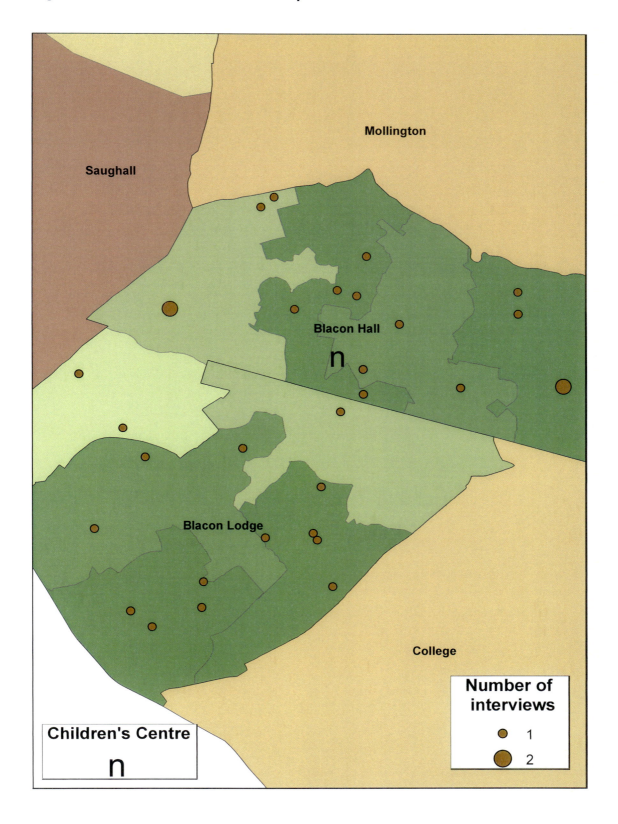

A number of strategies have been employed by the Sure Start programme in Blacon to increase the number of families who use services and to reach families who are not regular service users. These include linking new parents with active 'buddy' parents, road-shows (particularly at the local shopping parade), fun-days and the regular distribution of publicity material sent to registered families through the post. The provision of one-to-one services in the home has also been seen as one way of engaging with families who may not feel comfortable going out to a venue in the community to access a service. But despite efforts such as these, there is a view that Sure Start programmes may not be reaching those families who are most socially excluded and potentially those most in need (Gould, 2006). The fact that there are people who are not accessing Sure Start has led to both these families and the services being described as 'hard to reach'.

2.3 'Hard to reach' families

Since the early days of Sure Start, research in and about local programmes has examined aspects of programme reach and access for families who have not used services at all or who have had only occasional contact with Sure Start. This research into families who have not accessed services has often taken the approach of identifying different population groups who are 'hard to reach' (for example, Sure Start Higham Hill, 2004; Sure Start Bridlington South, 2003; National Evaluation of Sure Start, 2005). These groups have included parents with drug and alcohol problems, disabled parents, mother with postnatal depression, single mums, teenage mums, fathers, asylum seekers and refugees, families experiencing domestic violence, families where there are mental health problems, travellers, children with special needs and families from ethnic minority groups. A smaller number of studies have also identified working parents as hard to reach (for example, Sure Start Mexborough).

Although families in these groups may be over-represented in the population that have not accessed services because of, for example, their isolation, past experiences, physical needs or communication difficulties, families who do not fall into any of these groups may also be 'hard to reach'. It is, therefore, essential not to restrict the definition of 'hard to reach' to families who can only be described by certain characteristics as doing so may prevent the direction of resources towards other families who are also 'hard to reach' and in need.

A framework which reflects the breadth of those who are defined as the hard to reach population was developed by the National Foundation for Education Research (NFER) in their evaluation of the On Track programme (Doherty, Stott, & Kinder, 2004).

NFER identified three groups of 'hard to reach' families:

- 'minority groups' were defined as the traditionally under-represented groups. These were people who were often categorised according to 'population characteristics' such as minority ethnic groups, travellers and disabled people;

- 'slipping through the net' was the definition attached to people who are 'overlooked' or unable to articulate their needs. This group may include people who lack confidence or have difficulties or responsibilities that limit what they feel they can do;

- 'service resistant' was used to describe people who were unwilling to engage with services, 'the suspicious, the over targeted or disaffected' (Doherty, Stott, & Kinder, 2004, p.4). This group is seen as being wary of involvement or distrustful of service providers. The reasons for this may be as a result of their previous contact with statutory agencies or links to activities such as drug taking, alcohol abuse or criminal behaviour.

These three groups illustrate that 'hard to reach' is more than a demographic description of a group but, in addition, describes attitudes and behaviour and the concept should relate to the wider context of an individual's life experience. For each family, their decisions about accessing services may be a combination of a number of factors, including individual choice and contextual circumstances that are impacting on them at a particular point in time. The diversity of the population will be reflected in the reasons why families are not using services and, consequently, in the solutions that may encourage them to do so.

2.4   'Hard to reach' services

Some practitioners and authors prefer to describe the lack of engagement as one of hard to reach services rather than families who are hard to reach: it is also possible that the families concerned would be more likely to see services in this way. This perspective puts the focus on the factors which may make services more difficult to access for certain families, such as a lack of information, the timing of activities, transport difficulties, access to buildings, cultural insensitivity and the way that services

are presented to potential users. Some of these issues, particularly practical issues, were addressed in the National Evaluation of Sure Start study of the implementation of Sure Start programmes (NESS, 2005)

Chapter 3

Study design and methods

3.1 Introduction

This research starts from the premise that families who are amongst the population who are eligible to use Sure Start services but have not done so for at least six months are 'hard to reach'. The assumption is that some of the families who are not using services would benefit from a level of involvement or would wish to attend activities. It is impossible, however, to know which families are in this situation without speaking to all non-users.

3.2 The sample

The database at Sure Start Blacon holds both personal information about each local family who is registered with the Sure Start programme and routinely collected monitoring information which provides a picture of their use of services. The main sample for this research was drawn from the database of registered families, to include families who were currently eligible but who had not used any services for at least the last six months (between October 2005 and March 2006).

An interrogation of the Sure Start Blacon database found that there were 168 lead carers who had not accessed Sure Start for at least six months prior to March 2006 but who were eligible to do so. This list of non-users was checked by an administrative worker and a family support worker at the programme: 31 families were removed from the sample at this point because it was known that they had moved out of the area, recently used a service or were currently experiencing extreme difficulties which meant that an interview at this time was deemed inappropriate.

The remaining 137 families from the database comprised the main sample for the research. Each of these families was informed about the research by letter (see Appendix 2): the letter also contained an information sheet (see Appendix 3) and invited parents to arrange a specific appointment for an interview or to telephone if they did not want to take part in the research. An information sheet was also distributed to all Sure Start Blacon staff so that they knew about the research and would be able to answer any questions or redirect them to the research team at the University.

Over a four week period in April and May 2006, a total of 31 interviews were completed with registered non-users, a response rate of 23%. Following a minimum of two attempted contacts using a combination of letters, telephone calls, door knocking and the use of calling cards, 106 families were not interviewed. The reasons for the non-response are shown in Table 3.2.1.

Table 3.2.1   Reason for non-response

Reason for non-response	No. of families
Interview refused	17
No longer at this address or number unobtainable	46
No response to calls or visits	43

At the end of the interviews, any information gained about families who had moved, wrong numbers or telephone numbers that were unobtainable was passed to Sure Start Blacon so that they could update their database.

To supplement the sample from the database, two techniques were employed in an attempt to interview additional families.

The first method was to attempt to reach eligible families who did not use Sure Start services and who were not registered with the programme. Registered parents who were interviewed were asked if they had friends or family with young children who did not use Sure Start and who could be contacted: an information pack and pre-paid envelopes were left with four parents to pass on but no responses were received.

The second method was aimed particularly at younger parents (under 25 years old) as they were found to be under-represented in the sample of respondents. An analysis of the age of lead carers (usually mothers) in the total sample and the profile of mothers who were interviewed showed that the researchers were less likely to have been able to make contact with younger parents (under the age of 25 years) and where contact was achieved, they were less likely than older parents to agree to an interview. Contact was established with a local health visitor who agreed to pass on the information pack and pre-paid envelope: unfortunately, at the time of writing, the health visitor had been unable to distribute any of the packs.

3.3   The interviews

A research tool that had been developed by the author for a similar study in another Sure Start programme formed the basis of the structured interview schedule (Ward & Thurston, 2005). A small number of changes were made following discussions with the Sure Start Blacon programme manager.   The interview schedule is contained in Appendix 4. In addition to background information about the interviewee and their family, the schedule includes questions about their daytime routines, their knowledge about Sure Start Blacon and any activities they had attended. It then asked about factors that may inhibit service use and asked what might encourage them to attend in the future. The schedule then asked parents for their views on attending three existing activities – Song, Story and Rhymetime, the Pop In and adult education classes.

The interviews were conducted in the homes of the respondents by two senior researchers from the Centre for Public Health Research. Parents were asked to sign a consent form at the start of the interview (see Appendix 5).

3.4   Interview analysis

The quantitative data from the interviews was analysed on a computer package (SPSS). The majority of the information, however, was qualitative and this was analysed by coding then transferring the responses to the interview questions into charts which allowed for the exploration of different themes.

Throughout the report, quotations from the interviewees have been used to illustrate particular points. These quotations have been anonymised, although a unique interview number is attached to each one.

Chapter 4

Findings

4.1   Introduction

This chapter presents the findings from the interviews with parents. It starts with information about the families and their current daytime routines and then moves on to describe the families' knowledge about, and use of Sure Start Blacon activities. The factors that may inhibit service use are then described and possible solutions identified. The chapter concludes with parents' reactions to the idea of attending three existing activities – Song, Story and Rhymetime, the Pop In and adult education classes.

4.2   Family information

The interviews were conducted with 31 families, 30 of whom described their ethnicity as White British and one whose ethnic origin was unknown. All of the interviews were conducted with the mother, although fathers/partners were present on three occasions and contributed at times to the discussion. The information that is available suggests that only one of the interviewees was a lone parent.

Table 4.2.1 illustrates the age of the mothers who were interviewed as part of the research.

Table 4.2.1   Age of mother

Age of mother	No. of mothers interviewed
Under 20 years	1
20 to 24 years	2
25 to 29 years	4
30 to 34 years	13
35 to 39 years	8
40 years or over	3

It shows that the largest number of mothers interviewed were in the age band between 30 and 34 years old. In fact, mums in their thirties and forties accounted for 77% (24) of

the interviewees compared with 48% (65) of the non-users sample and 43% (151) of all lead carers registered with Sure Start Blacon (where age was known). However, attempts to interview a larger number of younger parents were unsuccessful, as discussed in Chapter 3.

The 31 families that took part in the research contained a total of 67 children, 33 of whom were of Sure Start age (under four years old). Two of the mothers interviewed were also expecting a baby. The age of all children in the families interviewed is shown on Table 4.2.2.

Table 4.2.2   Age of children

Age of children	Total no. of children
Less than 1 year	1
1 year	5
2 years	10
3 years	17
4 or 5 years	5
6 to 11 years	14
12 to 17 years	8
Aged 18 years or over	7

Although the majority of families contained only one child under four years old, four families had two children of Sure Start age. Out of the 31 families who took part in the research, 18 families contained at least one child of Sure Start age and children aged five years or older. Less than half of the interviewees, therefore, were solely parents of younger children and did not have children who were either at school or, in two cases, past school age.

In order to ascertain their familiarity with the area and whether they had been resident in Blacon when their younger children were born, respondents were asked how long they had been living in this part of Chester. As Table 4.2.3 illustrates, the majority of parents interviewed were longstanding residents of the area and 17 had lived in Blacon for more than 20 years. Only one family had lived in the area for less than two years

and all of the parents interviewed had been living in the Blacon Sure Start area when their youngest child was born.

Table 4.2.3   Time resident in the Blacon area

Length of time	No. of parents/carers
Less than 2 years	1
Between 2 and 5 years	7
Between 6 and 9 years	2
Between 10 and 20 years	4
More than 20 years	17

It is likely that the inability of the researchers to contact 46 potential interviewees because they were no-longer at the address that they lived at when they registered with Sure Start or their telephone number was unobtainable meant that the more mobile population formed a large proportion of non-response.

4.3   Current routines

The survey asked about the daytime routines of the pre-school children and their carers to gain a picture of the variety of things that the children were doing if they were not attending Sure Start activities.

4.3.1   Work and childcare

The majority of the 31 mothers who were interviewed (22, 71%) were employed or at college. Four of the mums worked or studied full-time whilst 18 worked on a part-time basis. Seven of the mothers who were in part-time employment worked only during the evening, night or at weekends whilst 11 were at work on a part-time basis during the day.

Whilst the women who were interviewed were at work, children were cared for by informal carers (fathers/partners, grandparents and an aunt), paid childcare (private nurseries, childminders and an after-school club) and via early education provision (school nurseries and a pre-school). As Table 4.3.1.1 illustrates, only four of the mothers who worked did not rely on partners or other family members for their

childcare. The table also shows that different sources of childcare were often combined to meet the needs of an individual family.

Table 4.3.1.1   **Childcare used by working mothers**

Type of childcare	No. of families
Father/partner only	9
Grandparents/aunt only	2
Private nursery/childminder only	2
Father/partner + grandparents	3
Father/partner + school nursery	1
Grandparents/aunt + private nursery/childminder	2
Grandparents/aunt + school nursery	1
Private nursery/childminder + school nursery	1
Pre-school + after-school club + school nursery	1

The research found that of the 31 families interviewed, only one had full-time childcare outside Blacon. In the 30 remaining families, the young children were in Blacon with parents, other family members or child carers for at least some of the time during the week.

4.3.2   School nursery and pre-school

The research found that 19 of the 27 children who were two or three years old accessed early education services at either a school nursery or pre-school.

A total of 15 children in 14 families attended a school nursery for five half day sessions each week. Thirteen of these children were three years old and two just reached their fourth birthday. In five of these families, mums worked part-time during the day and so in addition to the school nursery, children were also cared for by other family members, a childminder, and at a pre-school and an after-school club.

Five children attended pre-school groups in Blacon: mothers in four of these families worked part-time during the day and in three cases, other family members took care of these children outside of pre-school hours. The other child also attended a school nursery on a part-time basis.

4.3.3 Activities and groups

Respondents were asked about any organised groups or activities they attended with their children, both within and outside Blacon, that were not run by Sure Start.

The research found that eight of the children in the families interviewed attended an organised group activity during the week. Three children went to parent and toddlers groups with grandparents and two with their mothers: other activities mentioned were swimming lessons, a French class, a music class and Tumbletots. A number of reasons were given for attending these sessions rather than similar Sure Start activities. These were that the particular group was the choice of grandparents who took the child; that they had friends who went to the group; and that the days and times fitted in with their work and school dropping off and picking up routines. Just one of these activities took place in Blacon.

Some of the mothers who were interviewed specifically said that they had never looked into organised groups to attend with their children whilst others had tried them and found that their child was unhappy in that activity at the time. Four parents said they were just starting to think about looking for a suitable activity that their child could go to or they could attend with them.

4.3.4 Meeting with family and friends

Seven families referred to time spent during the week with family and friends, particularly those who also had younger children. Many of the mothers who were interviewed had grown up in Blacon and had family living locally. One interviewee also had caring responsibilities for a family member who lived nearby.

4.3.5 Time at home and household tasks

When asked about daytime routines, six respondents referred to time spent at home doing household tasks and 10 talked about child focussed activities in or around the home such as craft activities, playing, cycling, walks and play-centre or library visits. A number of parents also said that they spent time at home because their children were tired after nursery or pre-school or that they did not feel that their child needed to be at groups and activities everyday. Some of the parents who worked said that they just wanted to spend time alone with their children or needed to "*catch up with what needs doing*" (26a). There were, however, three mothers who were with their young children all day who did not attend any groups and did not describe any activities that they undertook with their children at home.

4.4 Knowledge about and use of Sure Start Blacon

All of the families who were interviewed as part of the research were registered with Sure Start Blacon: they all knew about Sure Start and had had some contact with the programme. During the interview they were asked how they first heard about the programme, what information they had received since then and any visits they had received or activities they had attended.

4.4.1 Getting to know about Sure Start

The majority of the mothers who were interviewed first heard about Sure Start Blacon when they were pregnant or soon after their children were born. Just over half of them (17) were told about Sure Start by a midwife or health visitor. Four of the respondents first heard about Sure Start Blacon from friends or by word of mouth, three heard via existing services (a school or parent and toddler group) and three received their first information about the programme when they were visited at home by a Sure Start worker.

4.4.2 Publicity and information

Since their initial contact with the local programme, all of the families interviewed could recall having received information about Sure Start activities through the post. They were generally positive about the style and content of the information but a third of the respondents said they now got less publicity information from Sure Start than they had done in the past. Two families assumed they were receiving less information because they had not attended any activities for a while.

Although the families who were interviewed were all similar in that they did not currently use Sure Start services, there was a range of opinion about the type and amount of information they would like. Some people received the information but admitted that it did not have any impact upon them for very different reasons, as illustrated by the following quotations taken from the interviews.

Two mums had never attended a Sure Start Blacon activity and appeared to be unlikely to do so in the future because they were not interested:

> 'I've had bits of things through the post but I just don't take much notice.' (2a).

> 'The information is fine but a lot of it doesn't really interest me.' (5a).

Another mum worked part-time but preferred to spend the time that she had with her daughter on her own. She said that she did not want to feel pressured into things but knew that Sure Start was there if she wanted it:

> 'Sending leaflets is ok but I don't want to be pestered to use activities.' (24a).

One respondent was surprised to be interviewed as part of the research. She worked part-time and had not realised that Sure Start was aimed at people like her because of her interpretation of how the service had been presented:

> 'The information gives the impression that Sure Start is for people who aren't working and single parents who need support or to develop skills … I'm not really aware of other things.' (23a).

Two other parents confirmed this impression, saying that the Sure Start information had little bearing on them simply because they worked:

> 'The information is ok but I work so it isn't relevant.' (30a).

> 'I don't take much notice of the information because I know I can't attend.' (17a).

Other parents, however, wanted more information about local services for children and families in general and information about Sure Start in particular, suggesting that they might use services in the future even though they do not do so now:

> 'I haven't had any information for a while – I'd like to be more aware of local activities.' (20a).

> 'I'm interested in getting information through the post – there might be something I am interested in doing.' (3a).

Two parents felt that whilst the publicity was generally good, some of it needed to contain more detailed information. This was mentioned with particular reference to the availability of a crèche alongside particular activities and the booking arrangements for crèche places.

4.4.3   Using activities and services

The information on attendance from the database was used to identify the families who had not used Sure Start Blacon services for at least six months. It showed that eight of the mothers who were interviewed last used a Sure Start service in 2003, 12 in 2004 and 11 last accessed Sure Start in 2005. For just under half of the families (15), the last service to be used was a weekly activity; for eight interviewees, it was a one-to-one or

home visit, for six the last activity attended was a special event or workshop and, for two families, it was a home safety equipment visit.

The interviews revealed that two families had recently started attending a Sure Start activity: one family now went to Song, Story and Rhymetime and another attended a Sure Start computer course where her child stayed in the crèche. The parent and child who now went to Song, Story and Rhymetime had previously attended in January 2005. They were recently able to rejoin when mum changed her working hours and were pleased to see that the same person was running the group. The parent who attended the computer course was last recorded on the database as attending a fun event in December 2003. In addition, two mums mentioned that, although they did not use Sure Start, their children currently attended activities with their childminders.

All of the parents who were interviewed were able to describe at least one contact with Sure Start Blacon, whether it was a home visit or attendance at an activity. Twenty-five respondents said that they had had a home visit from a Sure Start worker – a number of these were midwifery or health visitor visits but the mothers clearly associated them with the Sure Start local programme. The description of the other home visits showed that they were designed to introduce the family to Sure Start and/or provide advice on home safety.

The parents were generally very positive about the home visits. Comments were made about how friendly the staff were and how much information they had been given. One mum was particularly surprised by the nature of the visit:

> 'It wasn't what I expected – I'd been told they were like social workers checking up – they were very pleasant!' (2a).

One younger mum said she had found the home visits from the midwife, which she associated with the Sure Start programme, particularly beneficial:

> 'I liked the home visits ... I felt that she went out of her way for me.' (7a).

One parent, however, was put off by the Sure Start home visit:

> 'The Sure Start worker came just after he was born ... they gave me a safety pack and general information ... I felt that they were talking down to me, like not leaving the baby in the bath to open the front door.' (6a).

Seven of the parents who were interviewed said that they had not accessed any Sure Start activities and three parents had been to local activities with their children but they were not sure if they had been organised by Sure Start. Table 4.4.3.1 illustrates the Sure Start Blacon activities that the parents who were interviewed had attended.

Table 4.4.3.1   Sure Start services accessed by parents

Name of service	No. of families
Baby massage	6
Song, Story and Rhymetime	6
Pop In	5
Pre-birth experience	4
Breastfeeding group	4
Drop In	4
Adult learning	3
Fun days	2

During the interviews, some of the parents talked about their experience of Sure Start activities. A range of comments referred to their own and their child's experiences, their interaction with other parents and Sure Start workers, and feelings about the venue.

4.4.3.1 Mother and child experiences

Some parents spoke about the time that they attended a particular service. Baby massage was one of the most frequently accessed activities with six of the mums having tried it. This activity did not suit all of them: three parents spoke about the fact that they stopped going, one because *'my son hated it' (14a)*, another because her son *'screamed and I felt uncomfortable and people stared' (6a)* and a third because her child was often ill as a baby and she did not want to take him out too much.

Another mum, however, who had attended baby massage and other Sure Start activities, was very positive about the impact that Sure Start had had for her:

> *'I had postnatal depression after the birth and going to Sure Start activities really helped.' (21a).*

One parent said that her daughter really enjoyed attending Sure Start groups, particularly Song, Story and Rhymetime:

'I used to go to a lot of classes with my youngest – she is more confident – I think Sure Start helped in that.' (18a).

4.4.3.2 Group dynamics

A number of the mothers who were interviewed had felt somewhat excluded from the Sure Start activities they had attended. The Pop In and the Drop In seemed to be particularly problematic, although other activities were mentioned as the following quotations illustrate. All of these parents stopped attending each activity because they felt uncomfortable:

> *'The parents at the Pop In are clicky ... they don't let others in. I hated sitting by myself when my friend stopped going.' (12a).*

> *'I don't like the feeling from the regulars that you get when you go to the Drop In – they stare and I feel uncomfortable.' (6a).*

> *'I didn't feel like I was mixing at the (baby massage) group ... I find it difficult if the atmosphere is a bit thick ... it put me off trying anything else.' (15a).*

One parent felt that her situation was different from most of the other mums on the course and although it was not a problem for her on this occasion, she felt it could have been. She said:

> *'I enjoyed the course but found that other parents were from a different background and had a different attitude to life. I got over it because I enjoyed the course – they were friendly but I might have felt out of it with a different group.' (14a).*

Other parents, however, found that the groups could be very supportive as the following quotation illustrates:

> *'The breastfeeding support group was fantastic – I would have given up earlier if not for* (the worker) *and the group.' (17a).*

4.4.3.3 Sure Start workers

The parents were generally positive about the Sure Start workers and their role in groups and activities, even when parents were unsure about the session as a whole. One mum, who did not feel comfortable in the group, said the following:

> *'The staff at the Pop In were always chatty and offered you tea and fruit for the kids.' (12a).*

But despite the friendliness of the workers, this parent stopped attending the Pop In soon after her friend stopped because she felt excluded by the other parents. Another

parent, who was new to Chester, appreciated the role Sure Start staff played to encourage parents to go to activities. She said:

'It was nice that people were trying to get you involved.' (18a).

A third mum had attended the breastfeeding group with her baby and was very positive about the staff and the help she had received whilst attending the group:

'I really enjoyed it – the people who ran it were really good. With your first child it's reassuring to have people to help with advice.' (31a).

One parent, however, was put off Sure Start as a whole by a bad experience at a pre-birth class. This mum felt that some of the workers were patronising in the way that they challenged the decision she had made not to breastfeed her baby:

'I felt that because I had a mind of my own they didn't want to know… they need to realise not everyone will have their point of view.' (13a).

4.4.3.4 The venues

A small number of comments were made about the venues in which parents had attended Sure Start activities. One parent found the venue at Hatton Road too small and a bit claustrophobic whilst another said that the Pop In venue was *'a bit big and daunting.' (9a).* The library was seen as a pleasant venue for the Song, Story and Rhymetime activity and a number of parents who had observed a session, as it happened to be running at a time when they were visiting the library independently, were very positive about the activity.

Whilst some buildings may always be difficult for some people to get to, particular venues which had been convenient could also become problematic for parents if their circumstances change. One example is a parent who used to go to Song, Story and Rhymetime but who stopped once her older child started school nursery:

'I found I couldn't get to back to school in time from the library.' (18a).

4.5 Barriers to service use

During the course of the interview, respondents were asked a general question about the things that had stopped them from attending Sure Start Blacon activities, before being given a list of pre-set options against which they were asked to say the extent to which these reasons applied to them. The barriers to involvement suggested first by the respondents are shown in Table 4.5.1.

Table 4.5.1   Barriers reported by respondents

Reason for non-attendance	No. of parents/carers
Lack of time - work	11
- unspecific	3
Don't know anyone who attends	8
Prefer own routine	7
Feel uncomfortable/cliquey groups	6
Lack of information	5
Timing of activities, including school & nursery pick-ups	5
Child too tired/clashes with sleep routine	4
Inconvenient locations	3
Child too old/does things at nursery	3
Don't have things in common with mums who go	2
Have a family network	2
Bothered about other children's behaviour	1
Bothered about own child's behaviour	1
Lack of energy	1
Child too young	1
Activities aren't relevant to me	1
Attitude of staff (particular issue)	1

The reason most frequently given by interviewees for not attending Sure Start activities was a lack of time (mentioned by 41% of respondents) and, in the majority of these cases, this lack of time was related to employment.

Also important, however, was having someone to go with or knowing other parents who attend and, often linked to that, mums who were not comfortable in the groups or felt that there were cliques of parents who attended and it was difficult to join in if you went on your own. To illustrate this, two mothers said:

> 'I don't like the feeling from regulars when you go in – they stare and I feel uncomfortable.' (6a).

> 'I've never really started using Sure Start ... I don't know anyone in Blacon – I would probably go if I had friends that went.' (7a).

Seven parents, however, just wanted to be autonomous and simply preferred to work to their own timetables and do their own thing with their children, as illustrated by the following quotation:

> 'I don't want to work around their times. I'm very independent with my children and like to do things on my own with them. I prefer to fit in with my own routine.' (3a).

For some of these parents, this was specifically because they worked or went to college and had a limited amount of time with their children. One parent said:

> 'Now that we only have two days together, I prefer it to be just the two of us.' (31a).

A number of parents felt that once their child started attending pre-school or school nursery they did not need to attend Sure Start activities because their children were doing similar activities there. The timing of activities and picking up and dropping off children at school, nursery or pre-school was also problematic for some parents and others said that their children were too tired to attend another group once they had spent half of the day at pre-school or nursery. One finding of the research was that younger siblings may not have the same exposure to Sure Start as their older brothers and sisters because of the need to fit in with a different household routine as a result of the restrictions imposed by nursery and school drop-off and collection times.

Only one person said that they did not attend Sure Start activities because it was not relevant to her. This mum had two school aged children and a toddler aged 20 months but when asked what had stopped her going to Sure Start Blacon activities said one reason was that *'stuff doesn't really apply to me.'* (5a). This parent had, however, previously attended a computer class and had once contacted Sure Start for advice about her child's sleeping patterns: it may be that she was not interested or did not feel a need at this particular time or that other activities that she associated with Sure Start were not attractive to her.

After they had spoken about the things that had stopped them using Sure Start services, the parents/carers were asked to say whether any of a pre-set list of 12 hypothetical barriers were reasons that applied to them *'a lot'*, *'a bit'* or *'not at all'*. Figure 4.5.1 illustrates their responses.

Figure 4.5.1 Extent to which barriers applied to respondents

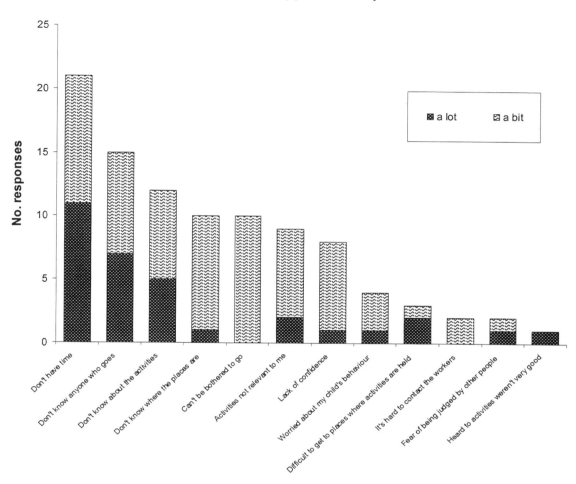

Barriers to service use

The results shows that, as when parents were asked an open question about what had prevented them from attending activities (Table 4.5.1), a lack of time was the most frequently mentioned factor given in response to the pre-set question: 68% (21) of the respondents said that a lack of time affected them 'a lot' or 'a bit'. Amongst these responses, it was the only barrier given for three respondents for quite different reasons: one mum worked full-time, one worked part-time and was at home on two mornings with her daughter and the other, whose son attended a school nursery, also had caring responsibilities for a disabled family member who did not live with them.

Not knowing anyone who goes was a factor for 48% (15) of the parents interviewed. The research also found that seven out of the eight mums who reported that a lack of confidence prevented them from attending Sure Start activities also said that not knowing anyone who goes was a major reason for their lack of involvement.

Although all of the parents interviewed were able to recall having received publicity about Sure Start Blacon activities at some time, 16 said that a lack of information about the activities and/or the venues was one of the factors that limited their use of services to some extent. Twelve parents said they did not know about the activities and 10 said that they did not know where the venues were.

Most parents did not report that difficulties contacting Sure Start workers was a factor that had restricted their use of Sure Start activities. The fact that Sure Start is based in the community wing at the local high school, an office which was felt by the programme to make staff somewhat inaccessible, was not a considered to have been important to most of the mothers who were interviewed.

One factor which emerged from the pre-set list of barriers that was not mentioned in the responses to the open question was that 10 mums admitted that 'can't be bothered' was a factor contributing to their lack of involvement in Sure Start. In response to the earlier question, only one parent had indicated anything like this saying that *a lack of energy'* (7a) was one of the factors that had restricted her use of Sure Start. In response to the pre-set list, parents were also more likely to say that Sure Start activities were not relevant to them, mentioned as affecting their attendance *'a bit'* by nine respondents.

4.6   Possible solutions

After talking about the things that had prevented them from attending Sure Start Blacon activities, parents were asked if there was anything that the programme could do which would make it easier for them to get involved.

Two-fifth of the respondents (13) did not feel that there was anything that Sure Start Blacon could do, a response that was qualified in a variety of ways. Five people were positive about Sure Start Blacon and the Sure Start workers but said that it was not something they were interested in and three people said they would go if they were interested in an activity or when their children were older. Another mum said that she had thought about whether there was anything that the programme could have done before to enable her to get involved but had come to the conclusion that there wasn't: another parent said it would be easier if mums could get to know each other but she did not feel that Sure Start could do anything about this. Only one parent said that a negative experience when attending one of the groups (where she felt overlooked

because she expressed her own opinion), meant that there was nothing that Sure Start could do to encourage her to try again. But even this parent said that it was 'a shame that one or two (workers) make you feel like that.' (13a) and later in the interview, did express an interest in knowing more about Song, Story and Rhymetime.

The remaining parents put forward a range of suggestions when asked what Sure Start could do to make it easier for them to attend another activity, particularly for the first time. As Table 4.6.1 illustrates, the suggestions referred largely to the timing of activities and the availability of information about them.

Table 4.6.1 Solutions to identified barriers

Solutions	No. of parents
Information about activities	9
Timing of activities	9
Venues	2
Introducing new people	1

The parents who referred to the difficulties they had with the timing of activities were usually doing other things during the day (including going to work) and were looking at the possibility of services in the late afternoon, evenings, weekends and during the school holidays. Specific comments related to the provision of adult education and antenatal classes in the evening and one-off events at weekends.

Parents who spoke about the provision of information said that they may be encouraged to use Sure Start if they had more information about activities and it was distributed on a more regular basis. Some people felt that if the information was distributed more regularly they would know that it was up to date.

The remaining suggestions related to the venues from which activities were run and getting to know other people. One parent said that the community centre would be a better location for activities for her and another said that she would be more likely to attend the Pop In if the venue was smaller as she found the current venue 'too noisy and a bit daunting.' (9a). This mum also said that Sure Start could encourage parents who did not know other families who attended a group by the provision of a 'greeter':

she had been put off by an experience of an activity where she said *'you go in and no-one says hello and shows you where things are.' (9a).*

4.7   Blacon Hall Children's Centre

The development of the children's centre should have an impact on the provision of services for young children and families in Blacon as there will be an identifiable venue where both workers and services can be accessed, as well as facilities that have been refurbished specifically for this client group. During the interview, parents were asked if they felt that having a children's centre building would make a difference to the use of Sure Start services by local families. The majority of the parents (23) did think that the presence of a building that was identifiable as a children's centre would make a difference to the use of Sure Start services by families in Blacon. The remaining eight respondents were evenly split between those who said it would not make a difference and those who were unsure.

Some of the benefits of the children's centre suggested by parents were a result of its specific location as it was closer than the current Sure Start venues to their homes (the location of the Blacon Hall Children's Centre in relation to the home addresses of the families interviewed is illustrated on Figure 2.2.3). Other people felt that it would be beneficial as parents would know exactly where to go if they wanted information about activities or wished to speak to someone. The parents who said that they did not think that a building would make a difference were largely concerned about the location, preferring to have services distributed more widely across the area. Only one parent said that having a building would put her off for other reasons. She said that:

> *'... it puts me off – I don't want to be with all those people – some round here look so rough.' (2a).*

4.8   Interest in existing activities

Three existing Sure Start Blacon services (adult education, the Pop In and Song, Story and Rhymetime) were described to the parents during the interview in order to illustrate the diversity of Sure Start Blacon's provision and to gauge the extent to which parents might be interested in attending activities in the future.

Of the 31 parents who were interviewed, five were certain that they were not interested in attending any of these activities in the future whilst the remaining 26 showed varying degrees of interest in one or more service. Figure 4.8.1 illustrates how many of the 26

parents expressed some interest in attending each of the named activities. It shows that, amongst this group of parents, Song, Story and Rhymetime and adult education courses generated more interest than the Pop In.

Figure 4.8.1   Interest expressed in specific Sure Start Blacon activities

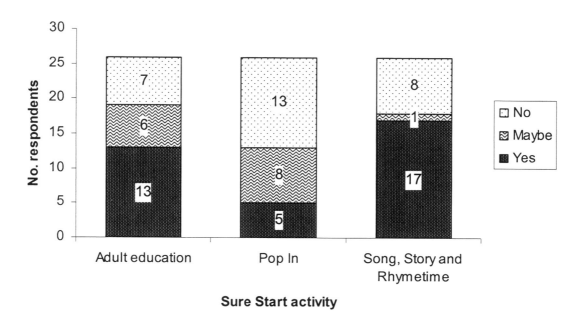

4.8.1   Adult education

Thirteen respondents said they were interested in attending Sure Start adult education courses and six said that they may be in certain circumstances. The topics of interest to the respondents ranged from mathematics and the NVQ in Childcare to recreational courses such as photography. Five parents said they were interested in learning more about computers, in part so that they understood more about what their children were doing at home and at school. First aid was another popular course, mentioned by three parents, one of whom had previously tried to get on a course at the hospital.

Parents linked the Sure Start adult education classes with their own employment and training opportunities. During the interviews, three parents specifically spoke about Sure Start adult education courses in relation to enhancing their employment prospects or returning to work. Other parents said they were not interested because they received training at work, were not planning to look for a different job, were already studying or were thinking about going to college or retraining when their children were older.

Those parents who were interested said that in order to attend Sure Start adult education classes, they needed more information (some said they did not know that Sure Start ran these courses), childcare that they could be confident that their child would settle in and two people felt they lacked confidence and would need encouragement (possibly being taken by a worker) to attend for the first time. The timing of the courses was also an issue, mentioned by seven people. Three of these parents said that early evening would be a good time for them to attend courses whilst one said that they would attend one-off adult education classes at the weekend.

4.8.2   Pop In

Only five parents said they were interested in attending the Pop In, usually as a convenient way to see a health visitor but also, for two parents, for the access it enabled to a parent and toddler group. One person saw it as a possible group for her mother to attend with her child. Another was interested in it solely as an opportunity for her 18 month old son to socialise with other children as the following quotation illustrates:

> 'I'll look at doing it for my son, not for me. I need to look at it in a different light.' (15a).

Conversely, other parents were not interested because they preferred to maintain contact with their own health visitor or they felt that their children did not need the parent and toddler group because they already attended a nursery or other activities where they mixed with other children of their own age. Four parents were hesitant or said they were not interested because they did not want to go to the Pop In alone: three of these parents had attended in the past and had felt that it was not as inclusive as it could have been.

4.8.3   Song, Story and Rhymetime

Of the three Sure Start Blacon activities that were described during the interview, Song, Story and Rhymetime was most positively received by the largest number of parents with more than half of the parents interviewed (17), saying that they would be interested in attending this group with their children. Three children did, in fact, already attend: one had joined recently, one went intermittently and another attended with his childminder.

Some of the parents who said they would be interested in Song, Story and Rhymetime were not currently able to attend because of the day and time that the group was held as it clashed with other routines or work: one parent actually went to a similar activity

elsewhere in Chester and said that she would change to Song Story and Rhymetime if it was held on a convenient day. Six parents were particularly positive about attending the group and requested more information about the activity: one person, however, who thought that her two year old son would enjoy the activity, said that she did not have the confidence to go to the group.

Three parents said they were not interested in this activity as their children did similar things at nursery. Another parent said it was not the right sort of thing for her child. Two parents said it was not the right activity for them, with one parent being quite clear about this:

> *'I'm not into craft activities – not prancing and dancing and singing with kids – no thanks!' (12a).*

One mother said that her partner, who cared for the children during the day, might go to a similar group if it were for dads and children but would not attend an activity that was solely attended by women.

4.9   Further contact and overall interest in Sure Start Blacon

At the end of the interview, parents were asked if they would like someone from Sure Start Blacon to contact them to tell them more about activities that they may be interested in. Table 4.9.1 illustrates their responses.

Table 4.9.1   Further information or contact with Sure Start

Response	No. of parents
No contact requested	8
Already in contact with Sure Start worker	1
Information through the post requested	14
Telephone contact or visit requested	8

The 22 requests for contact and/or further information, sometimes in relation to specific activities, were passed on to Sure Start Blacon soon after the interviews were completed in May 2006. In addition, 24 of the parents interviewed wished to receive a copy of the summary report from the Centre for Public Health Research when the research was completed.

Although the parents who were interviewed during the research were not asked about their overall interest in Sure Start Blacon and the likelihood of them getting involved in the future, an analysis of their responses to all of the questions suggests that the respondents fall into four groups:

- parents who are very unlikely to get involved;
- parents who may decide of their own volition to attend an activity at some point;
- parents who are likely to attend with a small amount of encouragement and more information;
- parents who appear to be quite isolated and would need more assistance in order to get involved.

Ten of the parents who were interviewed said or implied that they were unlikely to attend Sure Start Blacon activities in the future. The youngest children in eight of these families were aged three or just four years old: most of these parents were positive about Sure Start as a service for other families but not for them. In some cases this was a general lack of interest, as the following quotation illustrates:

'I think they are wonderful services for people who want them but there is nothing Sure Start can do to encourage me.' (13a).

In other cases, parents felt unable to use any Sure Start activities because they were not at home with their children during the week.

'What I have read and heard about activities is really good – it's just I work.' (11a).

'It was more useful when they were babies and I was not working and at home all day.' (18a).

One mother specifically thought that Sure Start had never applied to her because she worked:

'I think it's really good but aimed at people who haven't worked.' (14a).

Eleven parents said that they may attend a Sure Start Blacon activity in the future but this was often qualified by the fact that it would need to fit in with their pattern of work and other routines. Other qualifications were that their children would need to be older or, in the case of adult education, their attendance was dependent upon the particular courses that were offered.

Six parents were quite keen to get involved in particular Sure Start activities, although they said they would need more information and some may need a bit of encouragement before they will attend. Two of these parents had children who were now attending school nursery and solely interested in adult education courses for themselves. Three parents said they were interested in Song, Story and Rhymetime. One mum, who was looking for something for her one year old son said she would like to go and see what it was like and whether her son liked it. This mum said that she felt they were missing out and that she wanted to find a group they could attend *'to teach him things that I can't and help bring him on for school.' (25a).* The other parent in this group was in full-time work but was pregnant and hoped to work part-time after the birth and be able to use Sure Start services then.

Four of the parents that were interviewed as part of the research appeared to be quite isolated and could possibly derive great benefit from Sure Start if they were able to get involved. Three of these parents said they were interested in attending Sure Start activities but would find it difficult do so as the following quotations illustrate:

> *'It's hard going out on my own and meeting new people. I would go if I was with someone.' (16a).*

> *'I would be interested in* (adult education) *in the future – it's getting the confidence to go – I don't know how but I definitely will.' (29a).*

Two of these parents, however, requested a visit from the programme, one describing it as *'a first step'* and the other asked for further information through the post. One mum felt that Sure Start Blacon should have been more proactive in contacting parents who do not attend before this research:

> *'Sure Start should get in contact with people who haven't been for a long time – there has to be a reason why people stop going – maybe they don't have confidence or need encouragement.' (15a).*

The remaining parent said she would contact the programme if she wanted any further information but she also said that it is *'hard to get into a new group of people if you don't know anyone.' (7a).* In reality, it seemed as though this mum would need a more proactive approach from Sure Start but she did not ask for a visit or further information.

Chapter 5

Discussion

5.1 Introduction

This chapter investigates some of the key issues which emerged through the research. Firstly, it discusses the importance of data collection systems and ensuring that monitoring information is kept up to date. It then moves on to consider how provision such as Sure Start can influence parents' priorities and respond to the needs and time constraints of working parents. The chapter concludes by looking at a number of key issues for Sure Start Blacon and children's centres in general.

5.2 Knowing the local population

Although Sure Start local programmes developed as a geographically targeted response to meeting the needs of young children and their families, there is still great diversity in the population of any Sure Start area, both amongst families who are and those who are not using services. The findings from this research illustrate this diversity amongst families who did not use services provided by Sure Start Blacon. Amongst this group were families who had moved, those who were largely self sufficient, had other support networks or felt they had grown out of Sure Start, as well as families who appear to be isolated and could benefit from contact with the programme.

It is clear that in order to use resources efficiently and target provision most effectively to families who want or need services, registration information needs to be updated regularly and systematically. This will enable the identification of families who have moved out of the area and those who have moved locally so that they can receive information at their new address: these families may currently be confused with those who are hard to reach because they have not attended activities. Updated information could also highlight families who do not have specific needs and have indicated that they have particular reasons for not wanting to access Sure Start services so that resources could be concentrated on other people.

The research found that, at the present time, the fact that information is not up to date may have a disproportionate impact on the programme's ability to contact younger parents, as they appeared to be more likely than older parents to have moved to a new address since the date that they registered with Sure Start Blacon.

Mainstream workers who have ongoing contact with families, such as midwives, health visitors and school nursery teachers, could be valuable sources of information about the changing circumstances of the families with whom they come into contact. They could also be of assistance to local programmes in building up a 'needs profile' and identifying the people for whom services could be most beneficial at a particular point in time. There would need to be a commitment from a range of agencies and their staff for this to happen.

5.3   Understanding parents' priorities and changing behaviour

The premise of the research is that some of the families who are not attending Sure Start Blacon activities would wish to do so or their circumstances suggest that they would benefit from doing so. During the course of the research, four groups of parents were identified:

- parents who are very unlikely to get involved;
- parents who may decide of their own volition to attend an activity at some point;
- parents who are likely to attend with a small amount of encouragement and more information;
- parents who appear to be quite isolated and would need more assistance in order to get involved.

The question is whether Sure Start can facilitate a change in parents' behaviour and encourage them to do something that may be more beneficial to their babies and pre-school children's health and development than what they are currently doing. The research found that only a small number of parents attended any organised activities with their children: it is not that they are involved elsewhere in the sort of activities provided by Sure Start Blacon, rather that the majority do not attend organised activities at all.

Some parents were unlikely to get involved in Sure Start Blacon activities. Most of these parents wished to continue to receive information about Sure Start but said or implied that it was unlikely that they would attend anything in the future. The majority of these families had older children and they appeared to have 'grown out' of Sure Start or have never really become involved in the first place. Only one family in this group, whose youngest child was two years old, was quite defensive in the manner in which they said that they did not want or need Sure Start.

The remaining parents expressed some interest in going to one or more Sure Start Blacon activities during the interviews but were unsure about the service and/or lacked confidence to make the first move. Whilst 10 parents appeared to need more assistance, 11 parents appeared to be willing and able to get involved if they had more information, the activity was something that attracted them and it was held at a convenient time. In addition to the distribution of adequate information, the challenge for Sure Start local programmes is to present and promote activities so that these parents will choose to attend rather than do something else. To achieve this, the parents themselves will need to have identified, whether from friends or Sure Start publicity, a reason to get involved and to believe that attending an activity can help them achieve something they want for themselves or their children.

The research also found that some parents would need additional assistance from family, friends or Sure Start workers before they are able to turn this 'contemplation' about getting involved into action and actually using a Sure Start service. The degree of assistance required would vary as four of the mums appeared to be more isolated and seemed to require more assistance than the other six families.

5.4   Responding to working parents

The research also showed the impact that employment had on the lives of parents in Blacon as the majority of the parents interviewed worked or studied either full or part-time. The combination of work patterns within a household, often shift work and part-time employment, meant that parents' time spent with children is often fragmented and childcare and children's routines need a considerable amount of organisation or management.

The research found that while mothers were at work, the majority of child carers were grandparents and fathers who work shifts rather than childminders. Although some childminders attended Sure Start activities with the children they looked after, other carers did not. Mothers appeared to be reluctant to suggest to grandparents in particular that they take the children to activities, saying that they could not be expected to do this or that they would not like the group. Comments directly from fathers and also comments made by mums on their behalf suggested that they were averse to attending activities when there were not other men present. In order to provide play opportunities and social interaction for young children whose mothers

work, Sure Start Blacon would need to create conditions which encourage other carers to attend activities whilst the children are with them.

Some working parents were interested in services, particularly adult learning, that could be provided in the evenings and a small number felt that they had missed an opportunity because they worked during the day. But the majority of parents were unlikely to attend regular activities at this time of day. They saw evenings and weekends as family time, although some parents did say that they may be interested in one-off events, particular at weekends, if they also involved their children.

5.5 Programme priorities

In order to attract those families who need services the most, Sure Start Blacon may need to focus a larger proportion of its resources on families who are harder to reach. Greater priority would need to be given to practices which are designed to encourage and facilitate their engagement. These practices may include the identification of target groups, a new publicity strategy, increased liaison with mainstream services, outreach visits, befrienders and 'meeters and greeters' at activities.

5.5.1 Targeting

In addition to the targeting of individuals identified though having a greater awareness of the area's population, certain groups may also need to be prioritised. These include younger parents and older children who are not attending pre-school or school nursery provision, as well as parents generally who need more encouragement.

One important group that the research failed to contact in large numbers were younger parents, that is parents under 25 years old. They were more likely to have either moved since registration with Sure Start Blacon, or to refuse to be interviewed as part of the research. As age is the key factor with this group, these parents are more easily identified. Further work would be required to contact them in order to ascertain their situation and the extent and nature of their needs.

Parents of children who have reached the age of three or four years and are attending school nursery did not usually see the need to access Sure Start Blacon services either because they did not feel that their children needed additional opportunities for play or social interaction or that Sure Start activities duplicated things that they did at nursery. Sure Start Blacon may need to consider their objectives in providing services for

children of this age: it may be that provision should be targeted towards any three and four year olds who do not attend a school nursery. It is also clear that the parents of these children in particular did not seem to be aware of the wider Sure Start agenda and had not recognized that there were other services that Sure Start could offer to the family as a whole or to them as parents or to other child carers. Their understanding of Sure Start appeared to be solely in relation to provision for their children.

5.5.2 Information

Publicity and information are key elements of the strategy to attract the families who have been identified as the target population. The style and content of publicity is important so that parents identify with the Sure Start programme or children's centre and understand that the services are for people like them. There was quite a high level of awareness about Sure Start Blacon, but the interviews revealed that there was a need to keep people regularly informed. Parents had the impression that there had been less publicity about Sure Start Blacon activities in the recent past and they did not know whether the information they had last received was still current.

The research also found that although there was an overall preference for written information, this was not necessarily the case for the families who did not use services but appeared to be those most in need. These families required more than written information through the post to facilitate their engagement with Sure Start, as illustrated by comments made during some of the interviews, and the eight parents who said that they would like a telephone conversation or an outreach visit from a Sure Start Blacon worker.

5.5.3 Working with mainstream services

As discussed earlier, mainstream services could provide Sure Start Blacon with a wider and ongoing understanding of the needs of individual families within the local population. Their regular contact with a whole range of children and families is important as they may already be working with these families and can respond as needs are identified. There may be things that Sure Start can learn from 'brief interventions' techniques which have been used in the field of health. When successfully applied, brief interventions mean that a range of workers can take opportunities as they arise to identify needs, raise awareness and encourage involvement in appropriate services when people are ready to engage.

Evidence from this study suggests that some families will take a long time to access Sure Start and others may never do so. It is important for Sure Start to maintain a continuous (if low level) presence, in conjunction with mainstream services, so that when families want services they can easily access them. This should be easier when there is a more identifiable presence in the form of a children's centre building: the findings from the research supported this as the majority of parents felt that the children's centre would make it easier to contact Sure Start if they needed to.

5.5.4 Outreach and welcoming services

A major obstacle to the use of Sure Start Blacon services for some parents was their nervousness about going to an activity alone or being deterred by the fact that they thought that they would not know anyone once they got there. In some cases this was reinforced by the parent's previous experience of attending groups which they found 'cliquey' whilst in others, there was a more deep seated issue of lack of confidence, together with a degree of social isolation.

A number of the families who said they were interested in the programme appeared to want Sure Start to come to them in their own home before they would be able to make the first move. Outreach workers would need to provide the right sort of information to the parents, identify which (if any) activities interested them, and discuss what assistance Sure Start could provide to facilitate the family's access to these services. The interviews suggested that some people would need accompanying to activities whilst others would be reassured if they were certain that there would be someone at the group when they arrived who would make them feel welcome, introduce them to other parents and make it easier for them to become involved. Sure Start workers are the interface between new attendees and existing service users and have a key role in ensuring that activities are inclusive and accessible to all families.

The findings of the research suggested that some groups were easier for parents to attend for the first time. Groups such as Song, Story and Rhymetime appeared to be less threatening than activities such as the Pop In or Drop In. This may be because there is a structure to the activity that parents can fit into rather than having to manage their own integration into the group and it may be easier because the focus of the activity is on the child rather than the parent.

More structured groups may be a better setting to introduce some parents and be somewhere that they can build their own confidence and their confidence in Sure Start

as well as meeting other parents before moving on to activities that might have been more challenging to go to in the first instance. It is important that workers within all groups are aware when new parents attend and manage their introduction to the activity so that it is a positive experience and they are encouraged to come again.

Chapter 6

Conclusions

6.1 Introduction

This research with families who had not been in contact with Sure Start Blacon for at least six months provided a valuable insight into their lives, opinions and experiences: only by speaking to these families and others like them can Sure Start programmes begin to understand why some parents do not access their services and whether there are things that they can do to facilitate their involvement. The research is also useful preparation for the development of services from the children's centre where the core offer includes parental outreach and family support for 'those communities whose take up of services in the past has been low.' (Sure Start Unit, 2005).

This final chapter returns to the methodology employed by this study, the diversity of hard to reach families, a discussion of an 'acceptable' level of non-involvement and a brief reflection on the implications for children's centres in general.

6.2 The methodology and sample

In common with other Sure Start programmes, Sure Start Blacon has a system for the registration of children and families and for recording their use of services. This information was the starting point for the research in order to identify lead carers who had not accessed any Sure Start services for the previous six months. The use of this sampling frame, however, raises two issues.

The first concern is the level of registration with Sure Start Blacon as only half of the eligible families with children under the age of four years were registered with the programme in March 2006. Attempts were made to supplement this sample through snowballing from registered parents and contacts through a local health visitor but they did not result in any additional interviews.

The second issue was that some of the recorded information for at least one third of the families in the sample was out of date. Although letters were sent, these families could not be contacted because they had moved and/or their telephone number was unobtainable.

Although a sustained effort enabled the researchers to interview parents who could be categorised as hard to reach (families who are hard for services to reach are also hard to reach for research purposes), the parents who agreed to take part in the research were more likely to be older parents. This may have influenced some of the findings, particularly in relation to family structure and employment status. Younger parents, especially those under the age of 25 years, were either more likely to have moved from the address they lived at when they registered with Sure Start Blacon and so could not be contacted or, when they were contacted, were more likely to refuse to be interviewed. The decision was made by Sure Start Blacon not to offer parent's recompense for the time they spent being interviewed, such as the £5 shopping voucher which was used in a similar piece of research by the same authors (Ward & Thurston, 2005). It is impossible to know whether this would have made a difference to the response rate, particularly amongst younger parents, or whether a different, more community based, outreach approach is required to reach more families.

6.3 Diversity of families who are hard to reach

The findings of the research reveal the diversity of families who are hard to reach and the dynamic nature of this group. The situation of each family is different and is not static, shifting as the children grow older and circumstances such as the family structure, working hours and childcare arrangements change. It may mean that at certain times, for certain families, there are contextual factors which mean that services such as those provided by Sure Start can do little to facilitate their involvement. Children's centres will need to work with families at their pace and timing, seeing engagement not as a one-off event but a process which has phases when a family, because of other circumstances, is more or less likely to access services.

The starting point for the research was that the families were hard to reach because they were not accessing Sure Start activities but within each sample there was a broad spectrum of situations and experiences:

- some families who have attended in the past who will reappear of their own accord whilst others may need support and encouragement to do so;

- parents who may not have engaged in the past but expressed an interest in doing so in the future, whilst other families (who may or may not have particular needs) do not see Sure Start as something in which they want to be involved;

- there were families who did not take part in the research either because they refused to be interviewed, agreed to an appointment but were then unavailable or could not be contacted: these the families may be amongst those who are more intractably 'hard to reach'. Their circumstances and needs remain unknown.

Returning to the definition of 'hard to reach' taken from the NFER research (Doherty, Stott, & Kinder, 2004), it is clear that this research found families who would fall into each of their groups (minority groups, slipping through the net and service resistant) as well as individuals who do not have particular needs and have made a confident choice not to become involved in Sure Start.

6.4   An acceptable level of non-involvement

Although Sure Start programmes aim to provide a service to every family with young children in their catchment area, the process of involvement is a gradual one. Some people will have become involved early on whilst others will take a long time, and some will never engage with the programme. A proportion of families have made a choice not to become involved in Sure Start – for some that appears to have been a positive choice whilst for others there appears to be an element of resistance to the services offered by the programme. Whatever the circumstances, individuals have a right to choose not to become involved even if the service is aimed at bettering their own and their children's life chances.

The notion of hard to reach and the premise upon which this research was based could be seen as a professionally driven concept in that families are perceived as being in need of being reached or want to be reached but prevented from doing so as a result of individual predispositions or circumstances, or deficiencies in the services that are provided. Families, however, may not see themselves, their requirements or local services in this light and their lack of involvement may be much less calculated.

In order to meet the needs of all families in the local population, Sure Start might want to consider how to combine active recruitment (so that those parents who want or need to attend activities find it easy to become involved), with a continuous low level presence (so that families who have chosen not to participate can still contact the programme if they choose to do so). The research shows that the Sure Start programme does not necessarily need to reach all of the eligible population but it does

need to be aware of the families who want to or would benefit from access to their services.

6.5 The implications for Sure Start and Children's Centres

The findings of the research have implications for children's centres' access to families and families' access to the services they provide: some of the main points are highlighted below.

- **Database and monitoring**

  There is an ongoing requirement for an accurate database of children and families and monitoring systems to show who is accessing services.

- **Additional information**

  There is a necessity to record additional information which will identify families who are hard to reach and who want or need to participate.

- **Changing circumstances**

  This is a dynamic group whose circumstances change. Sure Start need to work with other agencies to maintain a clear picture of the population and to facilitate access.

- **A two way perspective**

  Sure Start need to see the situation from both the viewpoint of the agency and the family and to think in terms of both hard to reach families and hard to reach services.

- **Targeting**

  Services may need to be targeted towards families who are harder to reach, particularly younger parents, and a variety of methods used to try and engage them.

- **Presentation**

  Services need to be presented in a way that all local families with young children understand that they are applicable to them.

- **Always being there**

  Sure Start should maintain a low level presence even when families do not appear to want to be involved so that they know how to access services if they choose to do so

- **Striking whilst the iron's hot**

  Sure Start must ensure that the programme can respond to families when contact is achieved and when parents have shown some interest in activities.

- **Working parents**

  Sure Start must consider the needs of families in which parents work, including services that could be provided to fathers, grandparents and other people who care for their children during the day and whether there is a demand from working parents for particular activities in the evening and at weekends.

- **Services that are inclusive and welcoming**

  Sure Start needs to develop the role of workers who are at the interface between new attendees and existing service users so that new parents feel comfortable when they go for the first time.

References

ARC Research and Consultancy (2004). *Barriers to engagement.* Mexborough Sure Start. Retrieved June 12, 2006 from http://www.ness.bbk.ac.uk/ documents/findings/437.pdf

Cheshire County Council. (2006). *Local Statistics Metadata Catalogue: Deprivation.* Retrieved July 6, 2006, from http://www.cheshire.gov.uk/CheshireCC.Local Statistics.Web/MetaData/Deprivation.pdf

Doherty, P., Stott, A., & Kinder K. (2004). *Delivering services to hard to reach families in On Track areas: definition, consultation and needs assessment.* London: Home Office Development and Practice Report.

Gould, M. (2006). *Unsure Future.* Retrieved May 30, 2006 from http://www.SocietyGuardian.co.uk

National Evaluation of Sure Start. (2005). Implementing Sure Start local programmes: an in-depth study. Retrieved June 12, 2006, from http://www.ness.bbk.ac.uk/ documents/activities/implementation/861.pdf

Sure Start Bridlington South. (2003). *Evaluation of publicity and marketing.* Bridlington South Sure Start.

Sure Start Higham Hill. (2004). *Reaching hard to reach families: an evaluation for Sure Start Higham Hill.* Retrieved from http://www.ness.bbk.ac.uk/ documents/findings/834.pdf

Sure Start Unit. (2002). *A guide to planning and delivering your programme.* Retrieved October 2005, from http://www.surestart.gov.uk

Sure Start Unit. (2005). *A Sure Start Children's Centre for every community – Phase 2 Planning Guidance (2006-2008).* Retrieved October 12 2005, from http://www.surestart.gov.uk

Ward, F., & Thurston M. (2005). *Sure Start Hollinwood Outreach Survey.* Chester: Centre for Public Health Research, University of Chester.

Ward, F., Alford, S., Thurston M. & Pearson C. (2006). *Sure Start Blacon Reach Report, April 2004 – March 2005.* Chester: Centre for Public Health Research, University of Chester.

Appendix 1

Ranking of deprivation

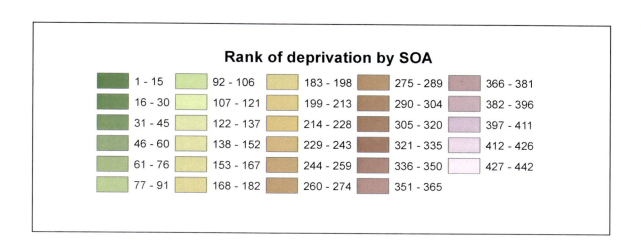

Rank of deprivation by SOA

1 - 15	92 - 106	183 - 198	275 - 289	366 - 381
16 - 30	107 - 121	199 - 213	290 - 304	382 - 396
31 - 45	122 - 137	214 - 228	305 - 320	397 - 411
46 - 60	138 - 152	229 - 243	321 - 335	412 - 426
61 - 76	153 - 167	244 - 259	336 - 350	427 - 442
77 - 91	168 - 182	260 - 274	351 - 365	

Appendix 2

Letter for respondents

April / May 2006

Dear

Sure Start Survey - tell us what you think!

We have been asked by Sure Start Blacon to do a survey of parents who do not use Sure Start services. We want to find out why parents don't go to Sure Start activities and see if there is anything the programme can do to encourage you to attend.

You have been chosen from the Sure Start database to take part in the survey. If you agree to take part a researcher from the University will visit you at home to ask you a few questions about services for parents with young children. If you would prefer to speak to us outside your home, let us know and we can book a room in a community building in Blacon. Anything you say to us will be treated confidentially and no names will be used in any reports we produce. The interview should take about 40 minutes.

Please ring Fiona Ward on Chester 512027 if you would like to arrange a time for us to come and see you: we can call in the early evening if you are working or are busy during the day. Otherwise, the interviewers will be in your area during the week beginning Monday ……………………………….. and will call to see you then.

When we call, we will have University id cards with a photo on which you can ask to see. If you do not want to take part, or if the person the letter is addressed to has moved, please let us know and we will not call.

There is more information about the survey on the other side of this letter.

We hope you can take part and are looking forward to speaking to you.

Fiona Ward / Frances Mann
Researchers

Appendix 3

Information sheet

More information about the survey ...

You have been invited take part in a survey. Before you decide it is important for you to understand why it is being done and what it will involve. Please read this sheet and ask if there is anything that is not clear or if you would like more information.

What is the survey for?

The survey is being done to find out what would encourage parents to use Sure Start activities. The information we collect from the interviews will be used to help Sure Start Blacon improve its services.

Why have I been chosen?

You have been chosen from the Sure Start Blacon database because you are a local parent who is registered with Sure Start but don't come to Sure Start activities at the moment.

Do I have to take part?

It is up to you whether or not you take part. If you decide to take part you will be asked to sign a form to say you have had this information about the survey. Even if you decide to take part, you can stop at any time and you don't have to give a reason. The interview will last about 40 minutes.

What are advantages and disadvantages of taking part?

You might enjoy telling us your views about what activities parents in Blacon really want for themselves and for their young children. We do not think there are any disadvantages in taking part in the survey.

Will my taking part be kept confidential?

Taking part in this interview is anonymous and no names or details that could identify you would ever be used in any reports.

What will happen to the results?

It is hoped that they will be used to improve and develop local services for young children and their families. A report will be written and that will go to the people who manage the Sure Start programme in Blacon.

Who is paying for the survey?

The survey is being paid for by Sure Start Blacon. Researchers from the University of Chester are doing the interviews and writing the report.

Who can I contact if I want more information?

If you would like to know more about the survey you can ring the researchers at the University of Chester – the researchers are Fiona Ward (01244 512027) and Frances Mann (01244 512059).

Appendix 4

Interview Schedule

Sure Start Blacon Outreach Survey

Spring 2006

1. How many children do you have and how old they are?

    Number of children ☐   Age of children ☐ ☐ ☐ ☐ ☐

2. How long have you been living in Blacon?

    Years ☐   Months ☐

3. Are you at home all day with your children or do you go out to work or college?

    At home ☐   Working ☐   College ☐

    a. *If working or studying*, is that full-time or part-time?

        Full-time ☐   Part-time ☐   Hours ☐

    b. *If working or studying*, who looks after your child/children for you whilst you are at work or college?

        ....

    c. *If child minded or at day-care,* Is this in Blacon?

        Yes ☐   No ☐

Thinking just about your child/children who haven't started school yet,

4. How much time do you have with your child/children during a normal week day?

    ....

    a. What do you do with your child/children during the day? Do you have a set routine? Are there things that you do or places you go every week?

        ....

        ....

        ....

    b. Are there things that your child /children do or places they go without you during the day?

        ....

        ....

Now I would like to ask you a few questions about Sure Start.

5. Do you remember how you first heard about Sure Start Blacon?

    ....

    ....

a. Have you received any other information about Sure Start Blacon since then?

Yes ☐   No ☐

b. *If yes*, do you remember what it was about and how you got it?

....

....

c. What do you think about all of the information you have had about Sure Start Blacon?

....

....

d. What do you think was the most useful information?

....

6. Have you used any Sure Start Blacon services?

Yes ☐   No ☐

a. *If yes*, what services or activities have you used?

....

....

b. What was the last service you used? When was that?

....

c. How did you get to hear about this service?

....

d. Was it what you expected? Why do you say that?

....

....

e. What has stopped you using Sure Start Blacon services since then?

....

....

7. Have you ever had a visit at home from a Sure Start worker?

Yes   ☐   No   ☐

a. *If yes*, how did you feel about the visit? Was it what you expected?

....

....

8. Taking everything into account, what would you say are the 3 main things that have stopped you from going to Sure Start Blacon activities?

1..

2..

3..

9. What do you think would encourage you to come to a Sure Start activity again?

....

....

10. Other people have suggested some reasons why parents may not use Sure Start services. Would you say that any of these reasons affect you either a lot, a bit or not at all?

	A lot	A bit	Not at all
Don't know anyone who goes			
Worried about my child's behaviour			
Can't be bothered to go			
Don't have time			
Not relevant to me			
Don't know where the place is			
Don't know about the activities			
Lack of confidence			
Fear of being judged by other people			
Difficult to get to the places where activities are held			
Heard the activities weren't very good			
It's too hard to contact the workers			

Interviewer: work through each thing ticked a lot or a bit above and ask about each in turn

You said that (*one at a time – if ticked a lot or a bit above*) might be a reason why you wouldn't come to an activity – is there anything Sure Start Blacon could do to make it easier for you?

1st thing...

2nd thing...

3rd thing...

4th thing...

5th thing...

11. From September this year, Sure Start Blacon will have a children's centre – that means they will have a building where parents can contact staff and where services for parents will be provided.

   a. Do you think the fact that there will be a children's centre building will make a difference to how you use Sure Start services?

   Yes [ ]   No [ ]

   b. Why do you say that?

   ....

   ....

   ....

12. I would like to ask you if you might be interested in 3 specific activities that Sure Start Blacon run – these are courses for adults, the Pop In and Song, Story and Rhyme Time.

Sure Start Blacon run courses just for adults on topics such as first aid, healthy eating, maths and English where a crèche is provided for children	
Do you think you would be interested in coming to this type of activity at any time in the future?	*If yes*, what would encourage you to come for the first time? *If no*, what would stop you?

The Pop In runs every week – it is like a parent and toddler group where children can play and parents can chat but it also has the services that you would normally find at a baby clinic.	
Do you think you would be interested in coming to this type of activity at any time in the future?	*If yes*, what would encourage you to come for the first time? *If no*, what would stop you?

Story, Song and Rhyme Time is a group for parents and children. As well as songs and stories, the weekly session includes art and crafts – the aim is for children to enjoy the activity whilst they talk and listen.	
Do you think you would be interested in coming to this type of group with your child at any time in the future?	*If yes*, what would encourage you to come for the first time? *If no*, what would stop you?

13. That is all of the questions I have to ask you. Is there anything else you would like to say about Sure Start Blacon?

....

....

....

Thank you very much for your time. The information you have given us is very important and will help Sure Start plan and advertise its activities.

- Would you like us to send you a copy of the report that we produce?

  Yes ☐   No ☐

- Would you like someone from Sure Start Blacon to contact you to tell you more about activities that you might be interested in?

  Yes ☐   No ☐

We need to speak to other mums with young children who live in Blacon but who do not go to Sure Start activities:

Do you know anyone else who we can speak to? If you do, could you pass on this letter and pre-paid envelop for us – we would really like them to take part in the survey as well.

Appendix 5

Consent Form

Study Number: 026

CONSENT FORM

Title of Project: **Outreach Survey – Sure Start Blacon**

Name of Researchers: Fiona Ward/Frances Mann

Please tick each box

1. I have read and understand the information sheet for the outreach survey and have had the chance to ask questions. ☐

2. I understand that my participation is voluntary and that I am free to withdraw at any time, without giving any reason. ☐

3. I agree to take part in the Sure Start Blacon outreach survey. ☐

---   -------------------------------   ---------------

Name of Parent   Signature   Date

---   -------------------------------   ---------------

Name of Interviewer   Signature   Date

Leave one copy with the parent/carer and interviewer takes the other